The Promises of Christmas

25 Advent and Christmas Reflections for All who Wait, Watch, and Wonder Once More

Other books by Stephen A. Macchia:

The Promises of Christmas

*25 Advent and
Christmas Reflections
for All who Wait, Watch, and
Wonder Once More*

STEPHEN A. MACCHIA

© 2018 by **Stephen A. Macchia**

Published by **Leadership Transformations**
P.O. Box 338, Lexington, MA 02420
www.leadershiptransformations.org

December 2018

Printed in the United States of America.

Library of Congress Cataloging-in-Publication Data
Macchia, Stephen A., 1956–
25 Fulfilled Promises / Stephen A. Macchia.

ISBN: 978-0-578-40217-8

Religion / Christian Life / Devotional

Dedicated to

Brenna Lynn Macchia
Papa's Joy

The Promises of Christmas

Table of Contents

The Promises of Christmas

INTRODUCTION

Welcome to the Advent and Christmas Journey!

Each year for the four Sundays prior to Christmas Day, we travel the same roads back to the manger and the first Advent of Jesus (the word advent is a derivative of the Latin word advenio which means coming or arrival). The Advent season is actually the "new year" of the church calendar and it offers all of us a fresh start to our life of faith and worship. Jesus' miraculous incarnation was not a "second thought" or "back up plan" in the heart of God. From the dawn of time, this was the promised and perfectly fulfilled plan of Almighty God.

Once more we embrace the seasons of Advent and Christmas. We look forward to all that awaits us in the coming weeks. We prayerfully prepare our hearts by opening ourselves to the transformative arrival of the Messiah. We anticipate with reverence and joy the worshipful reminders of the promised Light of the world. As darkness breaks forth into a new day of light, so does the arrival of Jesus dispel the darkness of this world by the infusion of good news. We follow the Advent pathway with gratitude, honor, and peace-drenched anticipation of the dawning of Christmas joy.

The way Jesus entered this world is no secret. You know the story. You've read it dozens of times. The narrative is nearly memorized, at least in your heart. The holy patterns we follow this time of year are pretty well established – in our families and in our congregations. Although accompanied by a busier than usual schedule of shopping, decorating, cooking, wrapping, organizing and traveling, it's also a time for solemn reflection. With growing anticipation we join the Church in preparing our hearts once more for the arrival of the Christ child, Who will transform our celebrations and renew our lives.

What I've noticed in my own travels to the manger, is how often I forget how well planned and how perfectly timed was the Incarnation. The world Jesus came to inhabit was ready and waiting, eager for the coming of the Messiah. Those who lived in the 1st Century Holy Land knew the ancient stories and oft-reflected prophecies, which for generations had been rehearsed over and over again. But, in so many ways, God's timing was indeed perfect, but many who were there live-and-in-person missed out on the fulfillment of the biggest, brightest, and best promise ever foretold.

So, for the next 25 days, as we approach the Advent of Jesus, we don't want to be among those who "missed it" by overt distraction or spiritual blindness. As we await once more the supernatural arrival of the Messiah, we're invited in the following pages to recall first the promise foretold in the Older Testament (spoken long ago by prophets like Isaiah and kings like David), and then the promise fulfilled in the miraculous and mysterious arrival of Jesus the Messiah. I've chosen 25 of my favorite promises; there are many others in the biblical text. But for this time around, herein are some of the gems selected for your prayerful consideration. May each set of readings and personal reflection experiences refresh and restore your soul.

As we approach the manger and rejoice in the coming of Jesus, we then enter into the 12 Days of Christmas. These days are designed to provide additional prayerful reflection so as not to forget the promises fulfilled in the delightful arrival of Jesus. We continue our Christmas journey all the way to Epiphany, a day of worshipful celebration and joyful gift giving as we recount together the heaven-directed visitation of the wise men to the humble manger home of Jesus, Mary, and Joseph. Suggestions for how best to engage in the 12 Days of Christmas are offered for your deliberation.

All of this is in prayerful, grateful and joyful anticipation of the Second Advent of Jesus, when he comes again in magnificent splendor, majesty, and glory. Then the things of this world, including our annual journeys to the manger, will be fond memories of times past. Then we will share eternity together as the family of God with our glorified Christ Jesus. Until that great day of magnanimous joy, the seasons of the church year will keep our hearts aflame with the light of his incarnation, joining our embrace of his cross-centered redemption and the unconditional gift of salvation and eternal life.

In the meantime, may this year's excursion through Advent and Christmastide be restorative and rejuvenating for you and yours. And, may you find yourself more-than-grateful for the well-timed execution of God's perfectly promised and delightfully fulfilled plan of salvation, redemption and eternal life in Jesus.

A blessed Advent, a Merry Christmas, and a joyful Epiphany to all.

In Christ's Joy,

Steve Macchia
Lexington, MA

PS Given the changing nature of the dates of Advent each new cycle of the church calendar year, this devotional is arranged instead around the month of December calendar, arriving at Christmas Day on December 25, followed by Christmastide, the 12 days of Christmas, and ending on Epiphany, January 6.

To all who participate in this prayerful journey, throughout this Advent and Christmas season, may you and yours...

Behold the fulfilled promises of Almighty God;

Believe the Gospel proclamation of Good News in the incarnate Jesus;

Belong to those who anticipate the coming Messiah with joyful celebration;

Become a faithful disciple who waits, watches, and wonders with Spirit-filled anticipation once more!

The Promises of Christmas

December 1 – Promise #1

The Messiah will be the seed of a woman

God's Promise Foretold – **Genesis 3:14,15**

So the Lord God said to the serpent, "Because you have done this, 'Cursed are you above all livestock and all wild animals! You will crawl on your belly and you will eat dust all the days of your life. And I will put enmity between you and the woman, and between your offspring and hers; he will crush your head, and you will strike his heel."

God's Promise Fulfilled – **Galatians 4:4, 5**

But when the set time had fully come, God sent his Son, born of a woman, born under the law, to redeem those under the law, that we might receive adoption to sonship.

Genesis 3 is known as the "first flicker of the gospel" - the protevangelium. Read this passage in context to discover the prophetic word as spoken directly to the serpent... the proclamation that the seed of a woman will eventually come to do battle with the serpent, the enemy of our souls. That seed is the Messiah Jesus, the One in Whom we wait, watch, and wonder once more. His Incarnation is the long-awaited miracle that the prophets foretold long ago.

Each of us faces a daily battle between flesh and spirit. It's been a reality since the dawn of time. But, in Jesus, the battle has been fought in our behalf and even though we struggle, we can rest assured that the victory over sin has been conquered once and for all in the arrival of our Messiah. As you embrace this Advent season and anticipate Christmas, what "battle in your soul" do you pray Jesus will reign over victoriously, and redemptively set you free from this "battle of the flesh" once and for all?

For your prayerful reflection…

_____

_____

_____

_____

_____

_____

_____

_____

_____

_____

_____

_____

_____

_____

_____

_____

*Lord Jesus, rule in my heart and mind today so that
whatever challenges I may face, I will be reminded of your
love and faithfulness. Amen.*

December 2 – Promise #2

The Messiah will be the descendant of Abraham, through whom all nations will be blessed

God's Promise Foretold – **Genesis 12:1-3; 22:18**

The LORD had said to Abram, "Go from your country, your people and your father's household to the land I will show you. 'I will make you into a great nation, and I will bless you; I will make your name great, and you will be a blessing. I will bless those who bless you, and whoever curses you I will curse; and all peoples on earth will be blessed through you." ...Abraham answered, "God himself will provide the lamb for the burnt offering, my son." And the two of them went on together.

God's Promise Fulfilled – **Acts 3:24-26**

For Moses said, "The Lord your God will raise up for you a prophet like me from among your own people; you must listen to everything he tells you. Anyone who does not listen to him will be completely cut off from their people.' Indeed, beginning with Samuel, all the prophets who have spoken have foretold these days. And you are heirs of the prophets and of the covenant God made with your fathers. He said to Abraham, 'Through your offspring all peoples on earth will be blessed.' When God raised up his servant, he sent him first to you to bless you by turning each of you from your wicked ways."

Abraham embodies "faithfulness" unlike many other biblical characters in the Old and New Testament. His fortitude, integrity, and open-handed obedience are remarkable graces to contemplate. His seed is a blessed and abundant seed, thanks to the faithfulness of God. Abraham confronted some of the most difficult tests, including God's command to sacrifice his son, Isaac. But, even then, he walked by faith, and not by sight.

Consider today the myriad ways God has proven himself to be faithful to you, even when you disobeyed or were tempted to look away from his invitation to trust.

In what way would your life look different today if you had the faith of Abraham, who withstood the presenting cultural pressures of his generation and focused his heart-filled intentions on loving, serving, and pleasing God above all else?

For your prayerful reflection…

_____

_____

_____

_____

_____

_____

_____

_____

_____

_____

_____

_____

_____

_____

Lord Jesus, please give me a renewed sense of your faithfulness, especially when I'm wavering in my trust today. Amen.

December 3 – Promise #3

The Messiah will be a willing sacrifice

God's Promise Foretold – **Genesis 22:1-18**

Some time later God tested Abraham. He said to him, "Abraham!" "Here I am," he replied. Then God said, "Take your son, your only son, whom you love—Isaac—and go to the region of Moriah. Sacrifice him there as a burnt offering on a mountain I will show you."

… The angel of the LORD called to Abraham from heaven a second time and said, "I swear by myself, declares the LORD, that because you have done this and have not withheld your son, your only son, I will surely bless you and make your descendants as numerous as the stars in the sky and as the sand on the seashore. Your descendants will take possession of the cities of their enemies, and through

your offspring all nations on earth will be blessed, because you have obeyed me."

God's Promise Fulfilled – **John 3:16, 17**

For God so loved the world that he gave his one and only Son, that whoever believes in him shall not perish but have eternal life. For God did not send his Son into the world to condemn the world, but to save the world through him.

Take a few moments and sit with Genesis 22, which recounts Abraham's complete surrender to God. Through the window of his willingness to sacrifice his son Isaac, the primacy of his love for God is realized. Few godly parents can relate to this story; most find themselves in utter dismay to consider such submission. However, Abraham remains for us an incredible example of godliness and open-handed love.

Note how your heart stirs within you as you consider how you would have handled such an amazing (and nearly impossible) request. Can you comprehend how difficult this must have been for a loving father to walk his son so close to his earthly demise? What does Abraham's submission remind you of today, as you hold fast to so many material, vocational, and even relational "possessions" which can bind your heart and hinder your soul from the full freedom of faithfulness?

For your prayerful reflection…

_____

_____

_____

_____

_____

_____

_____

_____

_____

_____

_____

_____

_____

_____

_____

_____

*Lord Jesus, your invitation to trust you wholeheartedly is
what I long for today. Amen.*

December 4 – Promise #4

The Messiah will be the Passover Lamb

God's Promise Foretold – **Exodus 12:1-51**

The LORD said to Moses and Aaron in Egypt, "This month is to be for you the first month, the first month of your year. Tell the whole community of Israel that on the tenth day of this month each man is to take a lamb for his family, one for each household…the animals you choose must be year-old males without defect, and you may take them from the sheep or the goats.

…On that same night I will pass through Egypt and strike down every firstborn of both people and animals, and I will bring judgment on all the gods of Egypt. I am the LORD. The blood will be a sign for you on the houses where you are, and when I see the blood, I will pass over you. No destructive

plague will touch you when I strike Egypt. "This is a day you are to commemorate; for the generations to come you shall celebrate it as a festival to the LORD—a lasting ordinance."

…The Israelites did just what the LORD commanded Moses and Aaron. At midnight the LORD struck down all the firstborn in Egypt, from the firstborn of Pharaoh, who sat on the throne, to the firstborn of the prisoner, who was in the dungeon, and the firstborn of all the livestock as well. Pharaoh and all his officials and all the Egyptians got up during the night, and there was loud wailing in Egypt, for there was not a house without someone dead.

…During the night Pharaoh summoned Moses and Aaron and said, "Up! Leave my people, you and the Israelites! Go, worship the LORD as you have requested. Take your flocks and herds, as you have said, and go. And also bless me."

God's Promise Fulfilled – **John 1:29, 36**

The next day John saw Jesus coming toward him and said, "Look, the Lamb of God, who takes away the sin of the world! This is the one I meant when I said, 'A man who comes after me has surpassed me because he was before me.' I myself did not know him, but the reason I came baptizing with water was that he might be revealed to Israel."

Then John gave this testimony: "I saw the Spirit come down from heaven as a dove and remain on him. And I myself did not know him, but the one who sent me to baptize with water told me, 'The man on whom you see the Spirit come down and remain is the one who will baptize with the Holy Spirit.' I have seen and I testify that this is God's Chosen One." The next day John was there again with two of his disciples. When he saw Jesus passing by, he said, "Look, the Lamb of God!"

Throughout the Older Testament, God instructed his people to repent of their sins symbolically through the sacrifice of their own livestock. The lamb's blood they placed on the doorways of their homes demonstrated their obedience. Moses' instructions to the people of God on the occasion of the first Passover was to last for future generations. Their repentance was to lead them into worship. When Jesus arrives as the ultimate Passover Lamb, the world of godly pursuit is turned upside down.

The redemptive work of Christ in all of our behalf is commenced in his Incarnation at Christmas. No longer are we to sacrifice animals for the forgiveness of our sins. Jesus' first coming and his sacrificial cruciform life is to prepare us for his Second Advent and our eternal "welcome home"! How are you preparing your heart to welcome and be welcomed by the Lamb of God, Jesus the Messiah?

For your prayerful reflection…

_____

_____

_____

_____

_____

_____

_____

_____

_____

_____

_____

_____

_____

_____

*Lord Jesus, thank you for your incarnation and your
willing sacrifice in my behalf. Amen.*

December 5 – Promise #5

The Messiah will be the star coming out of Jacob

God's Promise Foretold – **Numbers 24:17-19**

"The prophecy of Balaam son of Beor, the prophecy of one whose eye sees clearly, the prophecy of one who hears the words of God, who has knowledge from the Most High, who sees a vision from the Almighty, who falls prostrate, and whose eyes are opened: 'I see him, but not now; I behold him, but not near. A star will come out of Jacob; a scepter will rise out of Israel. He will crush the foreheads of Moab, the skulls of all the people of Sheth.' Edom will be conquered; Seir, his enemy, will be conquered, but Israel will grow strong. A ruler will come out of Jacob and destroy the survivors of the city."

God's Promise Fulfilled – **Matthew 2:2-6**

After Jesus was born in Bethlehem in Judea, during the time of King Herod, Magi from the east came to Jerusalem and asked, "Where is the one who has been born king of the Jews? We saw his star when it rose and have come to worship him."

When King Herod heard this he was disturbed, and all Jerusalem with him. When he had called together all the people's chief priests and teachers of the law, he asked them where the Messiah was to be born. "In Bethlehem in Judea," they replied, "for this is what the prophet has written:

" 'But you, Bethlehem, in the land of Judah, are by no means least among the rulers of Judah; for out of you will come a ruler who will shepherd my people Israel.'"

The brightest light in the starry sky would one day point the way to a humble manger scene where the offspring of Jacob was to be born. Shepherds noted the star in the sky as did the Magi...there was no confusion about the miracle the star had highlighted for all to see. Jealous King Herod would have nothing to do with honoring anyone who would be known as being born king of the Jews. But the Magi trusted the One who placed the bright star in the sky to lead them to the long awaited Messiah.

As you gaze upon the dark winter sky and note the brightest heavenly stars, give thanks to the Lord for the fulfillment of his promises to you, whether you are lowly of heart or a leader of households. The stars in the sky remain for us as symbols of the faithfulness of our awesome and majestic Messiah. His blessings, gifts, and promises fulfilled are as numerous as the stars he has placed for our amazement and delight. For what/whom are you most grateful this Advent season?

For your prayerful reflection…

_____

_____

_____

_____

_____

_____

_____

_____

_____

_____

_____

_____

_____

_____

_____

_____

_____

_____

Lord Jesus, fill me with your love as I gaze upon the beauty of the stars in the sky. Amen.

December 6 – Promise #6

The Messiah will be a prophet like Moses

God's Promise Foretold – **Deut. 18:15-19**

The nations you will dispossess listen to those who practice sorcery or divination. But as for you, the LORD your God has not permitted you to do so. The LORD your God will raise up for you a prophet like me from among you, from your fellow Israelites. You must listen to him. For this is what you asked of the LORD your God at Horeb on the day of the assembly when you said, "Let us not hear the voice of the LORD our God nor see this great fire anymore, or we will die."

The LORD said to me: "What they say is good. I will raise up for them a prophet like you from among their fellow Israelites, and I will put my words in his mouth. He will tell them everything I command him. I myself will call to account anyone who does not listen to my words that the prophet speaks in my name."

God's Promise Fulfilled – **Matt. 13:57; Luke 24:19**

Coming to his hometown, he began teaching the people in their synagogue, and they were amazed. "Where did this man get this wisdom and these miraculous powers?" they asked. "Isn't this the carpenter's son? Isn't his mother's name Mary, and aren't his brothers James, Joseph, Simon and Judas? Aren't all his sisters with us? Where then did this man get all these things?" And they took offense at him. But Jesus said to them, "A prophet is not without honor except in his own town and in his own home." And he did not do many miracles there because of their lack of faith. (Matthew 13)

~~~

Now that same day two of them were going to a village called Emmaus, about seven miles from Jerusalem. They were talking with each other about everything that had happened. As they talked and discussed these things with each other, Jesus himself came up and walked along with them; but they were kept from recognizing him. He asked them, "What are you discussing together as you walk along?"

They stood still, their faces downcast. One of them, named Cleopas, asked him, "Are you the only one visiting Jerusalem who does not know the things that have happened there in

these days?" "What things?" he asked. "About Jesus of Naza-
reth," they replied. "He was a prophet, powerful in word and
deed before God and all the people." (Luke 24)

God used Moses as a mouthpiece of the Almighty, a prophet to give voice to what he hears from listening obediently to the Lord. His words were life giving and restorative. Even though he initially resisted this call, his ultimate obedience led the people of God out of bondage and into the Promised Land. His prophetic voice proclaimed freedom and abundant life.

Jesus the Messiah, a member of the Triune God, was sent to earth to give voice to the Father's commands for his children. As the incarnate Son of God, his disciples were to listen to his words. Prophetic words are both stern and compassionate; they are truth and life. What are the words of life and love that you need to hear and heed today? If you listen for his voice in the Scriptures, prayer, and in the still small voice, will you choose to listen and obey?

For your prayerful reflection…

_____

_____

_____

_____

_____

_____

_____

_____

_____

_____

_____

_____

_____

_____

_____

Lord Jesus, give me ears to hear your voice and a heart that chooses to love and obey. Amen.

December 7 – Promise #7

The Messiah will be our Kinsman-Redeemer

God's Promise Foretold – **Ruth 4:4-17**

Meanwhile Boaz went up to the town gate and sat down there just as the guardian-redeemer he had mentioned came along. Boaz said, "Come over here, my friend, and sit down." So he went over and sat down.

Boaz took ten of the elders of the town and said, "Sit here," and they did so. Then he said to the guardian-redeemer, "Naomi, who has come back from Moab, is selling the piece of land that belonged to our relative Elimelek. I thought I should bring the matter to your attention and suggest that you buy it in the presence of these seated here and in the presence of the elders of my people. If you will redeem it, do so. But if you will not, tell me, so I will know. For no one has the right to do it except you, and I am next in line. I will redeem it," he said. Then Boaz said, "On the day you buy the land from Naomi, you also acquire Ruth the Moabite, the dead man's widow, in order to maintain the name of the dead with his property."

At this, the guardian-redeemer said, "Then I cannot redeem it because I might endanger my own estate. You redeem it yourself. I cannot do it."

...Then Boaz announced to the elders and all the people, "Today you are witnesses that I have bought from Naomi all the property of Elimelek, Kilion and Mahlon. I have also acquired Ruth the Moabite, Mahlon's widow, as my wife, in order to maintain the name of the dead with his property, so that his name will not disappear from among his family or from his hometown. Today you are witnesses!"

...So Boaz took Ruth and she became his wife. When he made love to her, the LORD enabled her to conceive, and she gave birth to a son. The women said to Naomi: "Praise be to the LORD, who this day has not left you without a guardian-redeemer. May he become famous throughout Israel! He will renew your life and sustain you in your old age. For your daughter-in-law, who loves you and who is better to you than seven sons, has given him birth."

Then Naomi took the child in her arms and cared for him. The women living there said, "Naomi has a son!" And they named him Obed. He was the father of Jesse, the father of David.

God's Promise Fulfilled – **Luke 1:50-58, 68-72**

And Mary said: "My soul glorifies the Lord and my spirit rejoices in God my Savior, for he has been mindful of the humble state of his servant. From now on all generations will call me blessed, for the Mighty One has done great things for me—holy is his name. His mercy extends to those who fear him, from generation to generation. He has performed mighty deeds with his arm; he has scattered those who are proud in their inmost thoughts. He has brought down rulers from their thrones but has lifted up the humble. He has filled the hungry with good things but has sent the rich away empty. He has helped his servant Israel, remembering to be merciful to Abraham and his descendants forever, just as he promised our ancestors."

...Mary stayed with Elizabeth for about three months and then returned home. When it was time for Elizabeth to have her baby, she gave birth to a son. Her neighbors and relatives heard that the Lord had shown her great mercy, and they shared her joy.

...His father Zechariah was filled with the Holy Spirit and prophesied: "Praise be to the Lord, the God of Israel, because

he has come to his people and redeemed them. He has raised up a horn of salvation for us in the house of his servant David (as he said through his holy prophets of long ago), salvation from our enemies and from the hand of all who hate us—to show mercy to our ancestors and to remember his holy covenant, the oath he swore to our father Abraham: to rescue us from the hand of our enemies, and to enable us to serve him without fear in holiness and righteousness before him all our days.

When Boaz redeemed Ruth from her forlorn circumstances, her life was turned upside down and inside out. There was no turning back. God plucked her up out of her forlorn condition and redeemed her in, for, by and through the love he made manifest in Boaz, her kinsman-redeemer. God redeems all who he loves, and the sending of Jesus his beloved Son was proof positive of his reconciling affection. The fulfillment of his promise to send a Redeemer came true.

All who follow God long for the redemption of the pain, heartache, suffering, and anguish we experience in our lifetime. How will you express your gratitude today for the myriad ways the Messiah Jesus has already redeemed your life from the pit and crowned you with love and compassion (cf. Psalm 103: 1-5)?

For your prayerful reflection…

_____

_____

_____

_____

_____

_____

_____

_____

_____

_____

_____

_____

_____

_____

_____

Lord Jesus, increase my faith and restore my life in the
fullness of your grace today. Amen.

December 8 – Promise #8

The Messiah will be a descendant of David, and will be greater than David

God's Promise Foretold – **2 Samuel 7: 1,4,12-16; Psalm 110:1-4**

"The Lord declares to you that the Lord himself will establish a house for you: When your days are over and you rest with your ancestors, I will raise up your offspring to succeed you, your own flesh and blood, and I will establish his kingdom. He is the one who will build a house for my Name, and I will establish the throne of his kingdom forever. I will be his father, and he will be my son. When he does wrong, I will punish him with a rod wielded by men, with floggings inflicted by human

hands. But my love will never be taken away from him, as I took it away from Saul, whom I removed from before you. Your house and your kingdom will endure forever before me; your throne will be established forever.' " (2 Samuel 7)

~~~

The LORD says to my lord: "Sit at my right hand until I make your enemies a footstool for your feet." The LORD will extend your mighty scepter from Zion, saying, "Rule in the midst of your enemies!" Your troops will be willing on your day of battle. Arrayed in holy splendor, your young men will come to you like dew from the morning's womb. The LORD has sworn and will not change his mind: "You are a priest forever, in the order of Melchizedek." (Psalm 110)

God's Promise Fulfilled – **Matthew 1:1, 22:42-45; Luke 1:32-33**

This is the genealogy of Jesus the Messiah the son of David, the son of Abraham....

...While the Pharisees were gathered together, Jesus asked them, "What do you think about the Messiah? Whose son is he?" "The son of David," they replied. He said to them, "How is it then that David, speaking by the Spirit, calls him 'Lord'? For he says, 'The Lord said to my Lord: "Sit at my right hand until I put your enemies under your feet." If then David calls him 'Lord,' how can he be his son?" No one could

say a word in reply, and from that day on no one dared to ask him any more questions. (Matt. 22)

~~~

In the sixth month of Elizabeth's pregnancy, God sent the angel Gabriel to Nazareth, a town in Galilee, to a virgin pledged to be married to a man named Joseph, a descendant of David. The virgin's name was Mary. The angel went to her and said, "Greetings, you who are highly favored! The Lord is with you."

Mary was greatly troubled at his words and wondered what kind of greeting this might be. But the angel said to her, "Do not be afraid, Mary; you have found favor with God. You will conceive and give birth to a son, and you are to call him Jesus. He will be great and will be called the Son of the Most High. The Lord God will give him the throne of his father David, and he will reign over Jacob's descendants forever; his kingdom will never end." (Luke 1)

If only we all could pick our ancestry. The long-awaited Messiah Jesus was a descendant of King David, once a shepherd boy, pulled from his family to lead the people of God as their king, a musician, psalmist, dancer, and oh yes, a sinner, adulterer, and liar too. Lest we get too carried away with how great was this man after God's heart, his line would ultimately reach to Jesus, One far superior to David, the perfect Messiah who would live among us to lead us redemptively into life eternal.

God promised that the Messiah would come from the lineage of King David, and he would surpass David in every respect. Although a great king, David was a human being. Jesus comes to reign as King, and does so with perfection. His heart and life, his witness and ministry, his words and deeds, were all in complete alignment with the Father. We wait, watch, and wonder once more as we anticipate the coming of Jesus as a perfect child. Will you follow Jesus today with fervency of heart and mind, knowing his perfect love will heal all your brokenness, including the brokenness of your family of origin?

For your prayerful reflection…

_____

_____

_____

_____

_____

_____

_____

_____

_____

_____

_____

_____

_____

_____

_____

_____

Lord Jesus, your perfect love is what I long for today as I notice the sins of those I love. Amen.

December 9 – Promise #9

The Messiah will be called God's Son

God's Promise Foretold – **Psalm 2:1-12**

Why do the nations conspire and the peoples plot in vain? The kings of the earth rise up and the rulers band together against the LORD and against his anointed, saying, "Let us break their chains and throw off their shackles." The One enthroned in heaven laughs; the Lord scoffs at them. He rebukes them in his anger and terrifies them in his wrath, saying, "I have installed my king on Zion, my holy mountain."

I will proclaim the LORD's decree: He said to me, "You are my son; today I have become your father. Ask me, and I will make the nations your inheritance, the ends of the earth your possession. You will break them with a rod of iron; you will dash them to pieces like pottery." Therefore, you kings, be wise; be warned, you rulers of the earth. Serve the LORD with fear and celebrate his rule with trembling. Kiss his son, or he will be angry and your way will lead to your destruction, for his wrath can flare up in a moment. Blessed are all who take refuge in him.

God's Promise Fulfilled – **Mark 1:11; cf. Luke 3:22**

At that time Jesus came from Nazareth in Galilee and was baptized by John in the Jordan. Just as Jesus was coming up out of the water, he saw heaven being torn open and the Spirit descending on him like a dove. And a voice came from heaven: "You are my Son, whom I love; with you I am well pleased."

"You are my son, whom I love; with you I am well pleased." These are the words that were amplified from heaven, God the Father to God the Son. The Spirit proclaimed these words for all to hear. The unmistakable presence of Jesus was declared and fulfilled in his perfectly human life. As he exits the waters of baptism, his commission is declared and salvation is offered to all who receive his loving presence, power and peace. From that place of blessing he enters the wilderness where for forty days he's tested and unscathed by the devil.

There is not a person alive today who doesn't long to know they are loved. It's the central message of life and when it's lacking there is a deep crevice in the heart. Any lacking of love can only be filled by God, the One who longs for us to know this truth in the deepest recesses of our soul. Do you know with certainty today that you are God's child, dearly and sincerely loved by God the Father? Do you know with certainty today that God is pleased with you, despite your sinfulness and the occasions where your rebellious heart emerges?

The gospel of Jesus is summarized in these words spoken by the Father. "You are my beloved child, in whom I am well pleased." Will you open-heartedly receive the unconditional love of Jesus? And, will you with generosity of heart offer the unconditional love of Jesus to all who cross your path today?

For your prayerful reflection...

_____

_____

_____

_____

_____

_____

_____

_____

_____

_____

_____

_____

_____

_____

Lord Jesus, may I receive your love and offer it graciously to all who cross my path. Amen.

December 10 – Promise #10

The Messiah will be the rejected cornerstone, and ultimately acclaimed

God's Promise Foretold – **Psalm 118:22-29**

The stone the builders rejected has become the cornerstone; the Lord has done this, and it is marvelous in our eyes. The Lord has done it this very day; let us rejoice today and be glad. Lord, save us! Lord, grant us success! Blessed is he who comes in the name of the Lord. From the house of the Lord we bless you. The Lord is God, and he has made his light shine on us. With boughs in hand, join in the festal procession up to the horns of the altar. You are my God, and I will praise you; you are my God, and I will exalt you. Give thanks to the LORD, for he is good; his love endures forever.

God's Promise Fulfilled – **Matthew 21:8-11, 42; cf. Luke 20:17-18**

A very large crowd spread their cloaks on the road, while others cut branches from the trees and spread them on the road. The crowds that went ahead of him and those that followed shouted, "Hosanna to the Son of David!" "Blessed is he who comes in the name of the Lord! Hosanna in the highest heaven!"

When Jesus entered Jerusalem, the whole city was stirred and asked, "Who is this?" The crowds answered, "This is Jesus, the prophet from Nazareth in Galilee."

…Jesus said to them [the chief priests and elders of the people in the temple courts], "Have you never read in the Scriptures: 'The stone the builders rejected has become the cornerstone; the Lord has done this, and it is marvelous in our eyes'?"

Imagine as a builder taking one of the most rejected stones on the pile to become the cornerstone of the building under construction. Not considered the brightest move to make from a builders perspective, but in essence that's exactly what God did in sending Jesus as the Messiah.

He knew full well that he would be followed, then flogged ...worshipped, then crucified...rejected, then acclaimed... all of Jesus offered all for love's sake, despite the rejection.

Advent offers us the opportunity to reflect upon our own view of Jesus. Do we question his authority in our world and in our lives, or do we acclaim him as sovereign over all? The Bible promises are replete with everlasting assurance that Jesus was indeed sent as Messiah. God followed through regardless of the world's acknowledgment of his presence and power.

The most important question lies at the doorpost of our hearts: Is the Jesus we await once more this Advent season, the One you want to know more intimately and follow more closely as your loving, grace-filled Messiah?

For your prayerful reflection…

_____

_____

_____

_____

_____

_____

_____

_____

_____

_____

_____

_____

Lord Jesus, I'm saddened by your rejection but gladdened by your acclimation. Rule in my heart today, and fill my soul with joy. Amen.

December 11 – Promise #11

The Messiah will be born of a virgin

God's Promise Foretold – **Isaiah 7:1,2, 10-14**

Then Isaiah said, "Hear now, you house of David! Is it not enough to try the patience of humans? Will you try the patience of my God also? Therefore the Lord himself will give you a sign: The virgin will conceive and give birth to a son, and will call him Immanuel."

God's Promise Fulfilled – **Luke 1:26-35; cf. Matthew 1:22-23**

In the sixth month of Elizabeth's pregnancy, God sent the angel Gabriel to Nazareth, a town in Galilee, to a virgin pledged to be married to a man named Joseph, a descendant of David. The virgin's name was Mary. The angel went to her and said, "Greetings, you who are highly favored! The Lord is with you."

Mary was greatly troubled at his words and wondered what kind of greeting this might be. But the angel said to her, "Do not be afraid, Mary; you have found favor with God. You will conceive and give birth to a son, and you are to call him Jesus. He will be great and will be called the Son of the Most High. The Lord God will give him the throne of his father David, and he will reign over Jacob's descendants forever; his kingdom will never end." "How will this be," Mary asked the angel, "since I am a virgin?" The angel answered, "The Holy Spirit will come on you, and the power of the Most High will overshadow you. So the holy one to be born will be called the Son of God."

Why would it be so important that the Messiah be conceived miraculously and birthed from a virgin's womb? This was the only way God could protect the unique status of the Messiah Jesus, for unless he was conceived supernaturally, born of a virgin, and delivered naturally into this world, he would be considered the son of a human father. And, scorned by those who would question his birth. God's choice was brilliant.

The miraculous and mysterious way Jesus was conceived is in direct fulfillment of God's loving promise to his people. His choice of a willing, humble, gracious virgin is such a delightful part of God's story. What do you make of the Spirit's implantation of human life into the womb of a young, innocent woman? The mystery and mastery of this single act is what brings many into a worshipful and trusting relationship with the Almighty. What is your prayerful response today?

For your prayerful reflection…

_____

_____

_____

_____

_____

_____

_____

_____

_____

_____

_____

_____

_____

_____

Lord Jesus, your coming to earth through the womb of a virgin is an unfathomable miracle of God's redemptive grace. I love and worship you, holy and miraculous Jesus. Amen.

December 12 – Promise #12

The Messiah will be a great light

God's Promise Foretold – **Isaiah 9:1-2**

Nevertheless, there will be no more gloom for those who were in distress. In the past he humbled the land of Zebulun and the land of Naphtali, but in the future he will honor Galilee of the nations, by the Way of the Sea, beyond the Jordan— The people walking in darkness have seen a great light; on those living in the land of deep darkness a light has dawned.

God's Promise Fulfilled – **Luke 1:76-79; cf. Matthew 4:13-16**

Zechariah [father of John the Baptizer] was filled with the Holy Spirit and prophesied…

"And you, my child, will be called a prophet of the Most High; for you will go on before the Lord to prepare the way for him, to give his people the knowledge of salvation through the forgiveness of their sins, because of the tender mercy of our God, by which the rising sun will come to us from heaven to shine on those living in darkness and in the shadow of death, to guide our feet into the path of peace."

The Light of the World has come in the life of Jesus. For those living in deep darkness, a bright light has dawned and the pathways that once were dimmed are now illumined. Jesus' foreteller John would prepare the way with a prophetic light of anticipation...Jesus would come as the Great Light. And both men's words of repentance would ready the hearer for the Kingdom of heaven, now all the nearer with the incarnation of the Messiah Jesus. Darkness was shattered by light and salvation arrived for all.

Each generation since the dawn of time has experienced darkness. Our day is filled with evidence of darkness, most powerfully represented in relational darkness. When will human suffering of all kinds cease to exist? Will you honestly repent, confess the corners of your own heart that are in darkness, and follow the light of Jesus with renewed fervency? Let his light shine in and through you today!

For your prayerful reflection…

_____

_____

_____

_____

_____

_____

_____

_____

_____

_____

_____

_____

_____

Lord Jesus, dispel the darkness of my heart today with your
heavenly light and love. Amen.

December 13 – Promise #13

The Messiah will be the Wonderful Counselor, Mighty God, Everlasting Father and Prince of Peace

God's Promise Foretold – **Isaiah 9:6-7**

For to us a child is born, to us a son is given, and the government will be on his shoulders. And he will be called Wonderful Counselor, Mighty God, Everlasting Father, Prince of Peace. Of the greatness of his government and peace there will be no end. He will reign on David's throne and over his kingdom, establishing and upholding it with justice and righteousness from that time on and forever. The zeal of the LORD *Almighty will accomplish this.*

God's Promise Fulfilled – **Luke 1:32-33**

In the sixth month of Elizabeth's pregnancy, God sent the angel Gabriel to Nazareth, a town in Galilee, to a virgin pledged to be married to a man named Joseph, a descendant of David. The virgin's name was Mary. The angel went to her and said, "Greetings, you who are highly favored! The Lord is with you." Mary was greatly troubled at his words and wondered what kind of greeting this might be. But the angel said to her, "Do not be afraid, Mary; you have found favor with God. You will conceive and give birth to a son, and you are to call him Jesus. He will be great and will be called the Son of the Most High. The Lord God will give him the throne of his father David, and he will reign over Jacob's descendants forever; his kingdom will never end."

By far the most familiar promise of Advent, the prophet Isaiah declares the gifts the Messiah will accompany upon his long-awaited arrival. He is Wonderful and awe-inspiring. He is the Great Counselor of the human heart. He is mighty in every regard. He is the God of all gods; everlasting and faithfully a Father to all in his family. He is the prince of peace and brings reconciliation to all who walk lovingly and graciously by his side.

Isaiah gives specific names to the Messiah that acknowledges his redemptive work in the hearts of all who follow him. Each of these names bear witness to the roles God delights to offer all who believe. Isaiah's prophecy declares the majesty the One true God would ultimately send in Jesus. The Son of God is fully God and in that truth we rejoice once more. What are the names of the Messiah, which mean the most to you today? Worship and adore him with all your heart!

For your prayerful reflection…

_____

_____

_____

_____

_____

_____

_____

_____

_____

_____

_____

_____

_____

_____

Lord Jesus, my heart rejoices in the many ways you lift my spirit with the reality of your powerful presence today. Amen.

December 14 – Promise #14

The Messiah will be called a Nazarene

God's Promise Foretold – **Isaiah 11:1-3**

A shoot will come up from the stump of Jesse; from his roots a Branch will bear fruit. The Spirit of the LORD will rest on him—the Spirit of wisdom and of understanding, the Spirit of counsel and of might, the Spirit of the knowledge and fear of the LORD— and he will delight in the fear of the LORD.

God's Promise Fulfilled – **Matthew 2:21-23**

So he [Joseph] got up, took the child and his mother and went to the land of Israel. But when he heard that Archelaus was reigning in Judea in place of his father Herod, he was afraid to go there. Having been warned in a dream, he withdrew to the district of Galilee, and he went and lived in a town called Nazareth. So was fulfilled what was said through the prophets, that he would be called a Nazarene.

There is no disputing the reality of Jesus' humble beginnings. Prophetically, Isaiah states that he will come forth from a shoot or root of Jesse. Jesse was the father of David, the lesser known of the two. In Hebrew, branch and Nazareth share the same consonants (other options for this prophecy are Psalm 22 and Isaish 53). His birth in a lowly manger bed in Bethlehem and his early life in the humble town of Nazareth are consistent with God's ways. Humble beginnings are good soil for the soul, and appropriate for the Messiah. No pomp and circumstance required. Nothing but humility, hiddenness, and holiness.

Our life with God is to be likened to the humble home of Jesus. We prefer riches, royalty, and the pomp and circumstance that accompany privilege. Not so with Jesus. The invitation of Advent is to reflect on our own lives and assess our intentionality during these holy days. Are you focused on the showcasing of your riches this season, or will you choose instead to generously and humbly serve others in Jesus' name?

For your prayerful reflection…

_____

_____

_____

_____

_____

_____

_____

_____

_____

_____

_____

_____

_____

Lord Jesus, today I choose the way of humility rather than the display of riches. Amen.

December 15 – Promise #15

The Messiah will be preceded by a forerunner

God's Promise Foretold – **Isaiah 40:3-5**

A voice of one calling: "In the wilderness prepare the way for the LORD; make straight in the desert a highway for our God. Every valley shall be raised up, every mountain and hill made low; the rough ground shall become level, the rugged places a plain. And the glory of the LORD will be revealed, and all people will see it together."

God's Promise Fulfilled – **Matthew 3:1-3; cf. Luke 3:1-6**

In those days John the Baptist came, preaching in the wilderness of Judea and saying, "Repent, for the kingdom of heaven has come near." This is he who was spoken of through the prophet Isaiah: "A voice of one calling in the wilderness,

'Prepare the way for the Lord, make straight paths for him.'"

John the Baptist was indeed that voice in the wilderness, the one who urged and invited all within earshot to open their heart and prepare for the coming Messiah. Repentance was his singular message, and the waters of baptism were his mode of response, but it was their hearts he was reaching for the Kingdom of heaven. It's always about the heart, first and foremost. Then, from the depth of the heart followers of the Messiah speak and act in accordance to his will.

Today, the voices of our commercial and competitive world are calling our name. Repentance has been relegated to the preacher and we bristle at the idea of being called to such a response. We much prefer the wide and easy road to the narrow and difficult way. However, during Advent we must attend to the voice of reason and the cry of desperation that exists in our world. What voices captivate your heart the most, and how will those voices point you back to the Messiah Jesus?

For your prayerful reflection…

_____

_____

_____

_____

_____

_____

_____

_____

_____

_____

_____

_____

_____

_____

Lord Jesus, tune my heart to hear your voice, even if the call is to repent of my unbelief or my disobedience to your better way. Amen.

December 16 – Promise #16

The Messiah will be a light for the nations

God's Promise Foretold – **Isaiah 42:1-7**

Here is my servant, whom I uphold, my chosen one in whom I delight; I will put my Spirit on him, and he will bring justice to the nations.

He will not shout or cry out, or raise his voice in the streets. A bruised reed he will not break, and a smoldering wick he will not snuff out. In faithfulness he will bring forth justice; he will not falter or be discouraged till he establishes justice on earth. In his teaching the islands will put their hope. This is what God the LORD says— the Creator of the heavens, who stretches them out, who spreads out the earth with all that springs from it, who gives breath to its people, and life to those who walk on it: "I, the LORD, have called you in righteousness; I will take hold of your hand. I will keep you and will make you to be a covenant for the people and a light for the Gentiles, to open eyes that are blind, to free captives from prison and to release from the dungeon those who sit in darkness."

God's Promise Fulfilled – **Luke 2:25-32 cf. Matthew 12: 15-18**

Now there was a man in Jerusalem called Simeon, who was righteous and devout. He was waiting for the consolation of Israel, and the Holy Spirit was on him. It had been revealed to him by the Holy Spirit that he would not die before he had seen the Lord's Messiah. Moved by the Spirit, he went into the temple courts. When the parents brought in the child Jesus to do for him what the custom of the Law required, Simeon took him in his arms and praised God, saying: "Sovereign Lord, as you have promised, you may now dismiss your servant in peace. For my eyes have seen your salvation, which you have prepared in the sight of all nations: a light for revelation to the Gentiles, and the glory of your people Israel."

Justice for all is the faithful light of Jesus, shining in the dark alleys of a lost and hurting world. The Messiah's voice is for all to hear, and it's a voice of reason, renewal, and reform. All who listen to him will find hope amidst the suffering and injustices of our day. This world so easily backpedals away from righteousness and impartiality, but in Jesus we lean forward with mercy, grace, and love.

Far too often the Christian community shirks its social responsibilities to the lost, the least, the lonely, and the left behind. We spend disproportionate time attending to our own needs and we neglect the glaring concerns of those who surround us with needs almost beyond our comprehension. When Jesus enters the world as the long-awaited Messiah, his work and witness focuses on those who were hungry, lost, forgotten, downtrodden, neglected, and hurting. In what corner of your own heart have you allowed prejudice, partiality, and pride to emerge? How will the justice and mercy of Jesus transform your response to others this Advent and Christmas season?

For your prayerful reflection…

_____

_____

_____

_____

_____

_____

_____

_____

_____

_____

_____

_____

_____

_____

*Lord Jesus, open the eyes of my heart to see the greater
needs that surround me, and lead me to serve others
generously in your name. Amen.*

December 17 – Promise #17

The Messiah will be called Emmanuel, God with us

God's Promise Foretold – **Isaiah 7:1,2, 10-14**

....Again the LORD spoke to Ahaz, "Ask the LORD your God for a sign, whether in the deepest depths or in the highest heights." But Ahaz said, "I will not ask; I will not put the LORD to the test." Then Isaiah said, "Hear now, you house of David! Is it not enough to try the patience of humans? Will you try the patience of my God also? Therefore the Lord himself will give you a sign: The virgin will conceive and give birth to a son, and will call him Immanuel."

God's Promise Fulfilled – **Matthew 1:20-23**

"Joseph son of David, do not be afraid to take Mary home as your wife, because what is conceived in her is from the Holy Spirit. She will give birth to a son, and you are to give him the name Jesus, because he will save his people from their sins." All this took place to fulfill what the Lord had said through the prophet: "The virgin will conceive and give birth to a son, and they will call him Immanuel" (which means "God with us").

The promise of the Messiah spans the Old Testament and the fulfillment is laced throughout the Gospels and the New Testament. The focus of the promise is Emmanuel, God is with us…he always has been, is today, and will be forever with us. Not only that, he's for us. He has our very best interests always in his heart and mind. As we wait, watch and wonder this Advent season, our receiving the loving embrace of the Incarnate Christ child becomes more resolute.

On this 17th day of December, recall the many ways God has been preparing all generations for the coming of Messiah, by always remaining with us, for us, around us, and in us. In the much beloved Advent hymn, "O Come, O Come, Emmanuel"* we are reminded of the many ways God has come to abide with us. Sit with these verses and be refreshed by the veracity of the biblical text as it comes alive in your heart.

O come, O come, Emmanuel (Isa. 7:14)

Rod of Jesse (Isa. 11:1), free us from Satan's tyranny victoriously;

Dayspring (Isa. 9:2), disperse gloomy clouds with cheers on high;

Key of David (Isa. 22:22), open wide the path to our heavenly home;

Lord of Might (Isa. 33:22), hold firmly the Law in majesty and awe;

Wisdom from on high (Isa. 11:2,3), invite order on the way to knowledge;

Desire of nations (Haggai 2:7), bind all people in one heart and mind.

Our hymn of praise exalts the heavens and blankets the earth.

O come, O come, Emmanuel...your prophets foretold the truth.

Wonderful, Counselor, Mighty God, Everlasting Father, Prince of Peace;

Emmanuel has come, is with us now, and will come again once more!

(*Additional reflections on the O-Antiphons noted in the Advent hymn, "O Come, O Come, Emmanuel" are provided in the Appendix for your prayerful contemplation from now until Christmas Day.)

For your prayerful reflection…

_____

_____

_____

_____

_____

_____

_____

_____

_____

_____

_____

_____

_____

_____

*Lord Jesus, as you are with me today, may I be ever
mindful of your presence and peace. Amen.*

December 18 – Promise #18

The Messiah will be the Suffering Servant

God's Promise Foretold – **Isaiah 52:13 – 53:12**

He grew up before him like a tender shoot, and like a root out of dry ground. He had no beauty or majesty to attract us to him, nothing in his appearance that we should desire him. He was despised and rejected by mankind, a man of suffering, and familiar with pain. Like one from whom people hide their faces he was despised, and we held him in low esteem. Surely he took up our pain and bore our suffering, yet we considered him punished by God, stricken by him, and afflicted. But he was pierced for our transgressions, he was crushed for our iniquities; the punishment that brought us peace was on him, and by his wounds we are healed...

God's Promise Fulfilled – **Matthew 8:14-17**

When Jesus came into Peter's house, he saw Peter's mother-in-law lying in bed with a fever. He touched her hand and the fever left her, and she got up and began to wait on him. When evening came, many who were demon-possessed were brought to him, and he drove out the spirits with a word and healed all the sick. This was to fulfill what was spoken through the prophet Isaiah: "He took up our infirmities and bore our diseases."

The Messiah was to be "despised and rejected, a man of suffering, and familiar with pain." The greatest Servant of all would become the One who suffered the most. Why would all of this become reality for our Messiah Jesus? Very simply: to declare his empathy for our suffering and to offer salvation from the infirmities of our broken hearts. As our long awaited Messiah he came to bear the curse of our diseases…to show his liberating love for all of his beloved disciples.

If you are a parent, you understand this concept: we would much rather suffer ourselves than have our child-who-we-love suffer. This is what the Father did for us in Jesus. What are the marks of suffering you are enduring as you await the loving embrace of our empathetic Jesus? How will you let Jesus heal, restore, and transform your heart?

For your prayerful reflection…

_____

_____

_____

_____

_____

_____

_____

_____

_____

_____

_____

_____

_____

_____

Lord Jesus, I await your coming in glory and am grateful for your gift of salvation. Amen.

December 19 – Promise #19

The Messiah will do life-affirming, redemptive deeds

God's Promise Foretold – **Isaiah 61:1-3**

The Spirit of the Sovereign LORD is on me, because the LORD has anointed me to proclaim good news to the poor. He has sent me to bind up the brokenhearted, to proclaim freedom for the captives and release from darkness for the prisoners, to proclaim the year of the LORD's favor and the day of vengeance of our God, to comfort all who mourn, and provide for those who grieve in Zion—to bestow on them a crown of beauty instead of ashes, the oil of joy instead of mourning, and a garment of praise instead of a spirit of despair. They will be called oaks of righteousness, a planting of the LORD for the display of his splendor.

God's Promise Fulfilled – **Luke 4:17-21**

Jesus went to Nazareth, where he had been brought up, and on the Sabbath day he went into the synagogue, as was his custom. He stood up to read, and the scroll of the prophet Isaiah was handed to him. Unrolling it, he found the place where it is written: "The Spirit of the Lord is on me, because he has anointed me to proclaim good news to the poor. He has sent me to proclaim freedom for the prisoners and recovery of sight for the blind, to set the oppressed free, to proclaim the year of the Lord's favor." Then he rolled up the scroll, gave it back to the attendant and sat down. The eyes of everyone in the synagogue were fastened on him. He began by saying to them, "Today this scripture is fulfilled in your hearing."

Offer good news to the poor. Bind up the brokenhearted. Proclaim freedom for all captives. Release prisoners from their darkness. Comfort all who mourn. Provide for those who grieve. Bestow a crown of beauty, oil of joy, and a garment of praise. Call them oaks of righteousness, a planting of the Lord for the display of his splendor. These are the deeds of the Messiah Jesus. For them. For us. For you and me. Each of them is outward in focus and sacrificial in provision. All of them are honored by God and acclaimed as worthy endeavors.

During Advent we are invited to consider the redemptive call of God, to participate in the releasing of captivity for those who are in bondage. Those who are enslaved by the worries, pressures, and concerns of this world are not in sync with the freedom and salvation found in Jesus. What abilities has the Lord bequeathed to you of late and what kind of redemptive service are you being called to render to another today?

For your prayerful reflection…

_____

_____

_____

_____

_____

_____

_____

_____

_____

_____

_____

_____

_____

*Lord Jesus, may I find the time to offer myself to
someone in need of the life-giving grace you so freely and
redemptively provide. Amen.*

December 20 – Promise #20

The Messiah will be born among sorrow and the object of a murderous plot

God's Promise Foretold – **Jeremiah 31:15**

This is what the LORD says: "A voice is heard in Ramah, mourning and great weeping, Rachel weeping for her children and refusing to be comforted, because they are no more."

God's Promise Fulfilled – **Matthew 2:13-18**

When they [the Magi] had gone, an angel of the Lord appeared to Joseph in a dream. "Get up," he said, "take the child and his mother and escape to Egypt. Stay there until

I tell you, for Herod is going to search for the child to kill him." So he got up, took the child and his mother during the night and left for Egypt, where he stayed until the death of Herod. And so was fulfilled what the Lord had said through the prophet: "Out of Egypt I called my son."

When Herod realized that he had been outwitted by the Magi, he was furious, and he gave orders to kill all the boys in Bethlehem and its vicinity who were two years old and under, in accordance with the time he had learned from the Magi. Then what was said through the prophet Jeremiah was fulfilled: "A voice is heard in Ramah, weeping and great mourning, Rachel weeping for her children and refusing to be comforted, because they are no more."

When the Magi outwitted Herod's wish to know the location of the baby Jesus, all the boys in Bethlehem under the age of two were ordered to be killed. Because of the Lord's protection, Joseph, Mary and Jesus fled for Egypt to escape the wrath of small-minded, jealous-hearted Herod. Jeremiah's words came true and weeping and mourning ensued with the death of innocent lives. How sad to realize such unfortunate evil would surround the joyous birth of the Messiah.

Our world is ravaged by suffering, violence, and injustice. We hear it on the news and we see it in our own lives. Why is it that the Lord would not see fit to end it all and miraculously cease the unnecessary suffering that surrounds and engulfs our world? Until the second advent of Christ we are destined to live in the turmoil of waiting and watching, working with God and remaining empowered by His Spirit to proclaim the redemptive message of hope in Jesus. How will you lovingly respond today?

For your prayerful reflection…

_____

_____

_____

_____

_____

_____

_____

_____

_____

_____

_____

_____

_____

Lord Jesus, I believe your faithful presence in our world is earmarked by the voice and actions of your people. May I be one such voice. Amen.

December 21 – Promise #21

The Messiah will be called out of Egypt

God's Promise Foretold – **Hosea 11:1**

When Israel was a child, I loved him, and out of Egypt I called my son.

God's Promise Fulfilled – **Matthew 2:13-15**

When they [the Magi] had gone, an angel of the Lord appeared to Joseph in a dream. "Get up," he said, "take the child and his mother and escape to Egypt. Stay there until I tell you, for Herod is going to search for the child to kill him." So he got up, took the child and his mother during the night and left for Egypt, where he stayed until the death of Herod. And so was fulfilled what the Lord had said through the prophet: "Out of Egypt I called my son."

Joseph was the human father God ordained to care for the baby Jesus and his mother Mary. Told by an angel in a dream to take his young family to Egypt for their protection, Joseph obeyed the Lord. When it was safe for their return, and on the heels of Herod's death, Joseph brought his little family back to Israel to live in Nazareth. Dreams. Angels. Prayers in the night. All these means were used of God to inform his beloved Joseph in the care of the Messiah Jesus. The pathway from Bethlehem to Egypt to Nazareth was the trail of blessing orchestrated by God. Thankfully, Joseph listened and obeyed.

It's remarkable to consider how intimately God protected the family of Joseph, Mary, and Jesus. His will was accomplished through supernatural means. The voice of God was abundantly clear and the manner in which Joseph chose to obey him is inspirational to all who have ears to hear. May his faithfulness be ours today and may you listen with an inclination to God's voice and the voices of faithful friends who seek a faithful life. Who has God given to accompany you in walking a life of faithfulness, grace, and love? How has God revealed his protection and grace?

For your prayerful reflection…

_____

_____

_____

_____

_____

_____

_____

_____

_____

_____

_____

_____

_____

_____

_____

*Lord Jesus, surround me with those who seek to listen and
obey you so I can do likewise. Amen.*

December 22 – Promise #22

The Messiah will be born in Bethlehem

God's Promise Foretold – **Micah 5: 1,2**

Marshal your troops now, city of troops, for a siege is laid against us. They will strike Israel's ruler on the cheek with a rod. But you, Bethlehem Ephrathah, though you are small among the clans of Judah, out of you will come for me one who will be ruler over Israel, whose origins are from of old, from ancient times.

God's Promise Fulfilled – **Matthew 2:1-6**

After Jesus was born in Bethlehem in Judea, during the time of King Herod, Magi from the east came to Jerusalem and asked, "Where is the one who has been born king of the Jews? We saw his star when it rose and have come to worship him." When King Herod heard this he was disturbed, and all Jerusalem with him. When he had called together all the people's chief priests and teachers of the law, he asked them where the Messiah was to be born. "In Bethlehem in Judea," they replied, "for this is what the prophet has written:

But you, Bethlehem, in the land of Judah, are by no means least among the rulers of Judah; for out of you will come a ruler who will shepherd my people Israel."

Bethlehem, the least of the clans of Judah, would become the birthplace of the Messiah Jesus. He would come to earth and declare the significance of the least, the lost, the lonely, the forgotten, the abandoned, and the ridiculed. It's no surprise that God would choose such a humble setting for the Savior and Redeemer to be delivered to this world. We often overlook the "least of these" whether in one's family lineage, home town, ethnicity, socio-economic background, or in any number of specific heritage markers. God chose the least of the least and he did so on purpose and in fulfillment of his promise.

Recall the time you realized you too were one of the least…perhaps it was when a friend reached out to help, or a word of hope was spoken to heal, or someone came alongside you to remind you of your worth. It's out of that awareness that we begin to see others who are lost and lonely, forgotten by this world, and in need of the love of Jesus. The fact of the matter is: Jesus came for the marginalized and offers them love. How will you choose to come alongside the "least of these" in your sphere of influence today?

For your prayerful reflection…

_____

_____

_____

_____

_____

_____

_____

_____

_____

_____

_____

_____

_____

_____

Lord Jesus, may your humble life of love and service
activate my love for others today. Amen.

December 23 – Promise #23

The Messiah's coming will be hopeful, prayerful and expectant

God's Promise Miraculously Fulfilled –
Luke 1:46-55

And Mary said:

"My soul glorifies the Lord
and my spirit rejoices in God my Savior,
for he has been mindful
of the humble state of his servant.
From now on all generations will call me blessed,
for the Mighty One has done great things for me—

holy is his name.
His mercy extends to those who fear him,
from generation to generation.
He has performed mighty deeds with his arm;
he has scattered those who are proud in their inmost thoughts.
He has brought down rulers from their thrones
but has lifted up the humble.
He has filled the hungry with good things
but has sent the rich away empty.
He has helped his servant Israel,
remembering to be merciful
to Abraham and his descendants forever,
just as he promised our ancestors."

Mary's song of praise is a prayerful response to the Lord's favor upon her life. Her willingness to serve God in the fulfillment of this miraculous promise is indicative of the condition of her heart. She is hopeful and expectant and she glorifies the Lord with mindfulness of his abundant blessing. She shouts for joy in the mercy extended to her as he so faithfully has done for generations prior to her life. She acknowledges the many ways God has remembered his promises and has lifted the humble, filled the hungry, and blessed the ones who extol his praise… and she joins the chorus.

As Christmas Day approaches, we are reminded of these beautiful words of Mary. Her heart is overflowing with praise to the Lord. Her awareness of her humble state is a tremendous reminder to all of us...it's only by the grace of God that we are who we are and we have what we have and we live how we live and we serve as we do. All of life is a gift, entrusted to us by the God who created, redeemed, and richly blessed us with abundance above and beyond all we could ever ask, dream or imagine. As you join the refrain of praise to the Lord, how are you rejoicing in God, the generously merciful lover of your soul? Offer your prayers of praise!

For your prayerful reflection…

_____

_____

_____

_____

_____

_____

_____

_____

_____

_____

_____

_____

_____

*Lord Jesus, I rejoice in your goodness and grace, bestowed
generously upon my life. Amen.*

December 24 – Promise #24

The Messiah's coming will be reason to praise, for salvation has arrived

God's Promise Mercifully Fulfilled – **Luke 1:68-79**

Praise be to the Lord, the God of Israel, because he has come to his people and redeemed them. He has raised up a horn of salvation for us in the house of his servant David (as he said through his holy prophets of long ago), salvation from our enemies and from the hand of all who hate us— to show mercy to our ancestors and to remember his holy covenant, the oath he swore to our father Abraham: to rescue us from the hand of our enemies, and to enable us to serve him without fear in holiness and righteousness before him all our days. And you, my child, will be called a prophet of the Most High; for you will go on before the Lord to prepare the way for him, to give his people the knowledge of salvation through the forgiveness of their sins, because of the tender mercy of our God, by which the rising sun will come to us from heaven to shine on those living in darkness and in the shadow of death, to guide our feet into the path of peace."

Zechariah's song reveals the heart of a godly father toward his loved ones. He praises the heavenly Father for unleashing his presence, power and peace over all who serve him. He praises the God of Israel for his work of redemption, salvation, holiness and righteousness. He recalls the promise of God to rescue his people from the hand of their enemies. And, he recounts the ways his son John would prepare for the arrival of Messiah Jesus to forgive sins and to guide the feet of his beloved into the pathway of peace.

This is a remarkable song of praise. A grateful and godly father giving voice to the inner recesses of his soul. The tenor of his song is one of glorious praise. His heart is full to overflowing and his words are delightful to behold. What would be the message of hope swelling from the depth of your soul as you recount the miraculous ways of God over your household and your heart? As your heart swells with Christmas joy, and the anticipation of gift giving mounts up, for what intangible gifts are you most grateful today, and to whom will you offer them this Christmas?

For your prayerful reflection...

_____

_____

_____

_____

_____

_____

_____

_____

_____

_____

_____

_____

_____

_____

_____

_____

Lord Jesus, I rejoice in you and give you all the thanks and praise, honor and glory, for the life you've so generously offered today. Amen.

December 25 – Promise #25

The Messiah has come to us as Jesus, the Name Above All Names

God's Promises Gloriously Fulfilled – **Luke 2:1-20**

In those days Caesar Augustus issued a decree that a census should be taken of the entire Roman world. (This was the first census that took place while Quirinius was governor of Syria.) And everyone went to their own town to register.

So Joseph also went up from the town of Nazareth in Galilee to Judea, to Bethlehem the town of David, because he belonged to the house and line of David. He went there to register with Mary, who was pledged to be married to him and was expecting a child. While they were there, the time came for the baby to be born, and she gave birth to her firstborn, a son. She wrapped him in cloths and placed him in a manger, because there was no guest room available for them.

And there were shepherds living out in the fields nearby, keeping watch over their flocks at night. An angel of the Lord appeared to them, and the glory of the Lord shone around them, and they were terrified. But the angel said to them, "Do not be afraid. I bring you good news that will cause great joy for all the people. Today in the town of David a Savior has been born to you; he is the Messiah, the Lord. This will be a sign to you: You will find a baby wrapped in cloths and lying in a manger."

Suddenly a great company of the heavenly host appeared with the angel, praising God and saying,

"Glory to God in the highest heaven,
and on earth peace to those on whom his favor rests."

When the angels had left them and gone into heaven, the shepherds said to one another, "Let's go to Bethlehem and see this thing that has happened, which the Lord has told us about."

So they hurried off and found Mary and Joseph, and the baby, who was lying in the manger. When they had seen him, they spread the word concerning what had been told them about this child, and all who heard it were amazed at what the shepherds said to them. But Mary treasured up all these things and pondered them in her heart. The shepherds returned, glorifying and praising God for all the things they had heard and seen, which were just as they had been told.

The birth narrative is a miraculous glimpse into the coming of Messiah Jesus into this world. Born in a humble manger, with Mary and Joseph by his side, he brings with him good news of great joy for all the people. Today is the day the Messiah comes as a baby, and is surrounded by a great company of the heavenly host. The angels song is very simply, "Glory to God in the highest heaven, and on earth peace to those on whom his favor rests." The shepherd's song is also filled with glory and praise.

But Mary treasures the moment, the pondering this new reality in her heart. In the midst of the hustle and bustle of this amazing season of the year, perhaps there will be a moment or two for you to devote to pondering the awesome gifts offered to you in Jesus. God's promises have all been delightfully fulfilled in the presence of Jesus. On this Christmas Day, how are you cherishing the miraculous gifts of the Incarnate Christ-child, our loving Messiah Jesus?

For your prayerful reflection…

_____

_____

_____

_____

_____

_____

_____

_____

_____

_____

Merry Christmas, and may you and yours…
Behold *the fulfilled promises of Almighty God.*
Believe *the Gospel proclamation of*
Good News in the incarnate Jesus.
Belong *to those who anticipate the coming Messiah*
with joyful celebration.
Become *a faithful disciple who*
waits, watches, and wonders with Spirit-filled
anticipation once more! Amen!

December 26 – January 6

The Twelve Days of Christmas

Christmastide Blessings

Happy Christmas to all!

Christmas day is traditionally known as the beginning of "the twelve days of Christmas" concluding on January 6, which is called Epiphany. During the 12 days of Christmas, we join the chorus of Christ followers in commemoration of those who so faithfully loved Jesus the Messiah.

For many of us, when we consider the Twelve Days of Christmas we think of the festive song of the same name. Tradition invites us to think of these in light of important Christian doctrines. Perhaps this is why it was used for many to teach children their beliefs. According to an online article found on Beliefnet (beliefnet.com/faiths/Christianity.aspx), what follows is a list of the days and their corresponding Christian meaning;

The partridge in a pear tree represents Jesus, referenced as a partridge, who sacrifices its life to save its young;

Two turtle doves is a reference the Old and New Testaments;

Three French hens denotes faith, hope, and charity, or the three gifts of the wise men;

Four calling birds are the four evangelists, Matthew, Mark, Luke, and John;

Five golden rings are the first five books of the Old Testament;

Six geese a-laying refer to the six days of creation described in Genesis;

Seven swans a-swimming represent the seven gifts of the Holy Spirit (wisdom, understanding, counsel, strength, knowledge, piety, and fear of the Lord);

Eight maids a-milking are the eight Beatitudes;

Nine ladies dancing are the nine choirs of angels (Seraphim, Cherubim, Thrones, Dominions. Virtues, Powers, Principalities, Archangels, and regular angels); or the nine fruit of the Holy Spirit (love, joy, peace, patience, kindness, goodness, faithfulness, gentleness, and self-control);

Ten lords a-leaping are the Ten Commandments;

Eleven pipers piping are the 11 faithful Apostles;

Twelve drummers drumming represent the twelve points of belief in the Apostles Creed.

Whether you trust this traditional view of the light-hearted Christmas song or not, it's rather witty to consider this creative approach to teaching children doctrinal beliefs that matter to one's faith development.

However, those who ascribe to the 12 Days of Christmas and await these days with prayerful anticipation, are to be respected. This was not my experience growing up, nor is it our family's expression today. But, I have come to honor this season as a significant part of the Advent-Christmas-Epiphany expression.

Christian History Magazine offers a wonderful take on the importance of the Twelve Days of Christmas ("The Real Twelve Days of Christmas" by Edwin and Jennifer

Woodruff Tait, Issue 103, pages 25-27), which I commend. Here are some notable paragraphs worthy of your prayerful reflection...

"If we look a bit deeper into Christian history, we discover that Christmas Day itself ushers in 12 more days of celebration, ending on January 6 with the Feast of the Epiphany. More than just lending their name to a cryptic holiday song, the real 12 days of Christmas give us a way of reflecting on what the Incarnation means in our lives."

"The three traditional feasts (dating back to the late fifth century) that follow Christmas Day reflect different ways in which the mystery of the Incarnation works itself out in the body of Christ. December 26 is the Feast of St. Stephen – a traditional day for giving left-overs to the poor (as described in the carol ' Good King Wenceslas'). As one of the first deacons, Stephen was the forerunner of all those who show the love of Christ through their generosity to the needy. But more than this, he was the first martyr of the New Covenant, witnessing to Christ by the ultimate gift of his own life."

"Commemorated on December 27, St. John the Evangelist is traditionally thought to be the only one of the 12 disciples who did not die a martyr. Rather, John witnessed to the Incarnation through his words, turning Greek philosophy on its head with his affirmation, 'The Word was made flesh, and dwelt among us' (John 1:14, KJV)."

"On December 28, we celebrate the Feast of the Holy Innocents, the children murdered by Herod after the birth of Jesus (Matthew 2:16). These were not martyrs like Stephen, who died heroically in a vision of the glorified Christ. They were not inspired like John to speak the Word of life and understand the mysteries of God. They died unjustly before they had a chance to know or to will – but they died for Christ nonetheless. In them we see the long agony of those who suffer and die through human injustice, never knowing that they have been redeemed. If Christ did not come for them too, then surely Christ came in vain. We renew our faith that the coming of Christ brings hope to the hopeless. And, in the most radical way possible, we confess that, like the murdered children, we are saved by the sheer mercy of Christ, not by our own doing or knowing."

Finally, on Epiphany (January 6), the celebration of Christmas comes to an end. On this day we primarily commemorate the visit of the Magi with their gifts of gold, frankincense and myrrh; we also celebrate the baptism of Jesus; and, we remember his first miracle of turning water into wine. The season of Advent has ushered in the celebrations of Christmastide, which comes to a glorious conclusion at Epiphany. It commemorates the beginning of the proclamation of the Gospel – Christ's manifestation to the nations.

From Advent, Christmas, and Epiphany, we turn our attention to the life and teachings of Jesus. We recommit ourselves once more to faithful living and loving and learning. We acknowledge the Incarnation of Jesus, we celebrate his coming into this world and into our hearts, and we lean fully into what it means to live fully committed to his teachings as ones who are lovingly redeemed and continuously transformed.

In Jesus the Word became flesh, and dwelt among us… we behold his glory and we proclaim it to a lost and needy world. Thanks be to God!

~~~~~

During the 12 Days of Christmas, consider the promises of God and recount the many blessings he has bestowed upon you in this life. Here are a few prayerful ways to spend quiet time during the next twelve days:

December 26 – in light of the tradition of remembering St. Stephen, what are the tangible and intangible gifts you most treasure and the gifts you most delight to share with others?

_____

_____

_____

_____

December 27 – as the Church remembers the life and ministry of St. John the Evangelist, what are the words that give your heart life and light, and offer encouragement, hope and joy in the Lord? With whom will you share these words today?

_____

_____

_____

_____

December 28 – the injustice of untold number of children killed at the edict of Herod is baffling and disheartening to consider. What are the injustices that surround you today, and how is God inviting you to prayerfully and/or practically work toward relieving such suffering?

_____

_____

_____

_____

December 29 – the memories of time spent with family and friends over the holidays continue to resonate in your heart and mind. What were the shared experiences of this past Christmas that you are most grateful for today?

_____

_____

_____

_____

December 30 – the lights and decorations of Christmas are resplendent with beauty. As you ponder the meaning of Christmas and Jesus, the Light of the world, how have you seen Christ evidenced in the eyes, voice, heart, and actions of others this week?

_____

_____

_____

_____

December 31 – as the year comes to an end, this is your final opportunity to write a check for your local church or a favorite charitable organization. How will you practice God-honoring generosity today?

_____

_____

_____

_____

January 1 – New Year's Day is a great time to reflect back over the past year with gratitude to God for the myriad gifts he gave to you over the past 12 months. What are the highlights of last year for which you are most thankful today?

_____

_____

_____

_____

January 2 – take time to prayerfully examen your life with God (examen is an ancient spiritual formation practice designed to help you look back with gratitude, notice God's presence in your life, attend to your emotions, and pray into the days ahead). What do you sense are the new invitations from God for the year ahead (consider the health of your relationships, the clarity of your vocation, your exercise routine, your service to others, your generosity, etc.)?

_____

_____

_____

_____

January 3 – the vibrancy of your spiritual life is key to the vitality of your soul. In the coming months you may wish to spend more time alone with God in silence and solitude, reading the Scriptures, conversing with God in prayer, and reflecting on your daily journey of faith. How will the year ahead be reshaped in your personal prayer life?

_____

_____

_____

_____

January 4 – others are undoubtedly counting on you for tangible and intangible support, words of encouragement, prayerful attentiveness, time together, and acts of service. As you consider your priority relationships, what needs can you tend to specifically, and perhaps even without recognition?

_____

_____

_____

_____

January 5 – the beauty of God's creation surrounds you and beckons your attention. As you peruse your surroundings, both the natural and human-made signs of beauty, how is your heart quickened to rejoice in the Creator?

_____

_____

_____

_____

January 6 – today we conclude our reflections with Epiphany, the day we commemorate the gifts of the wise men, gold, frankincense, and myrrh. What are the gifts God has given to you in this season of life and how will you enhance those gifts (training, additional practice) and share them abundantly with others?

_____

_____

_____

_____

Behold the fulfilled promises of Almighty God.

Believe the Gospel proclamation of Good News in the incarnate Jesus.

Belong to those who anticipate the coming Messiah with joyful celebration.

Become a faithful disciple who waits, watches, and wonders with Spirit-filled anticipation once more!

The Promises of Christmas

Appendix

Additional Reflections on the O Antiphons of "O Come, O Come, Emmanuel"

Advent hymns speak to the longing in our hearts for the coming of Christ. We sing them each year during this holy season, embedded with rich and deep significance for all. By far one of the most popular, and my personal favorite, is "O Come, O Come, Emmanuel" with 7 grand stanzas. Each verse known as one of the "O Antiphons." Each of the 7 "antiphons" depict 7 "types" of Christ presented to us prophetically in the Old Testament and fulfilled in the first Advent of Christ's incarnation recorded in the New Testament. God's promises...fulfilled.

The term "antiphon" literally means "opposite voice" or "responsorial voice" as would occur between a choir and congregation, a call and response. From one to another, the voices call out from side to side, back and forth, to and from. The Antiphons in this hymn are filled with "alternating" voices of meaning, from the Old to the New Testaments, from the prophecies foretold of Christ to the fulfilment thereof. From the prophetic not yet to the present already and onward to the future not yet…a groaning of sorts in anticipation of Christ's coming, in His incarnational arrival as a child, and in His future coming in yet-to-be-revealed glory. The antiphonal voices of the prophets are joined responsively by the king himself, Jesus, and his faithful disciples then and now.

This ancient hymn was originally penned in Latin in the 12th century (Veni, Veni Emmanuel). The version most often used today was translated into English in 1851 by John Mason Neale and includes three more verses.

The hymn was inspired by the traditional O Antiphons sung at Vespers services during the final seven day stretch of Advent. An antiphon (from the Greek anti + phon meaning opposite + voice) refers to a call and response mode of singing. The seven O Antiphons are comprised of a title for the Messiah from the prophet Isaiah: O Sapienta (Wisdom), O Adonia (Lord), O Radix Jesse (Root of Jesse), O Clavis David (Key of David), O Oriens (Rising Sun, Morning Star, or Day-Spring), O Rex Gentium (King of Nations), and O Emmanuel (God with us).

A fascinating fact from the O Antiphons is that the titles for the Messiah in reverse order Emmanuel, Rex, Oriens, Clavis, Radix, Adonia, Sapienta form an acrostic ERO CRAS in Latin, which is translated "I will come tomorrow." Those monks who wrote and arranged the lyrics to the O Antiphons married theological and artistic creativity in a fabulous way. We will consider one of the antiphons each day prior to Christmas Eve.

Day 1 – Traditionally read on December 17 – Emmanuel

O come, O come, Emmanuel, and ransom captive Israel

That mourns in lonely exile here, until the Son of God appear.

Rejoice! Rejoice! Emmanuel shall come to thee, O Israel.

This first "type" of Christ, foretold in Isaiah and revealed in the gospel of Matthew, is Emmanuel. The "with us" God is prophesied and fulfilled in Christ Jesus. He came to us in the flesh as a baby boy, and He comes to us and abides with us as Emmanuel. His coming sets the captives free, provide companionship for the lonely, and ongoing hope for all who mourn in places of exile and wandering from God.

Invite Jesus to come into the inner recesses of your heart today to set you free, provide intimate companionship, and convert your anxiety into hope.

Day 2 – Traditionally read on December 18 - Wisdom

O come, O Wisdom from on high, who orders all things mightily

To us the path of knowledge show, and teach us in her ways to go.

Rejoice! Rejoice! Emmanuel shall come to thee, O Israel.

The second "type" of Christ is Wisdom, also predicated by Isaiah in chapter 11, "The Spirit of the Lord will rest on Him – the Spirit of wisdom and of understanding, the Spirit of counsel and of might, the Spirit of the knowledge and fear of the Lord – and He will delight in the fear of the Lord."

We cry out to the Lord, "Come" – "Yes, come even more!" we pray. Come alongside us and abide "with us" and offer to us "wisdom" from on high, and teach us to walk the well ordered path of your will.

O Come, O Come, Emmanuel. It's a joy to rejoice in You!

Day 3 – Traditionally read on December 19 – Lord of Might

O come, O come, thou Lord of might, Who to Thy tribes on Sinai's height

In ancient times didst give the law, in cloud and majesty and awe.

Rejoice! Rejoice! Emmanuel shall come to thee, O Israel!

In Exodus 3 we see how the angel of the Lord came to Moses in the burning bush, invited Moses to lead the people of God out from their slavery in Egypt and give them the Law, both of which would set them free. The Lord works mightily in their midst and behalf, all of which resounds with shouts of rejoicing and praise. In the Incarnation, Jesus Himself fulfills the Law and comes to set us free!

Let your heart cry out to the Lord today, inviting his strength to reside within you as you face various trials, tribulations, and temptations. Look for the burning bush of his presence there to guide, protect, lead and sustain you. Be free from the inside out as you offer prayers of majesty and awe to Almighty God.

Day 4 – Traditionally read on December 20 – Rod of Jesse

O come, O Rod of Jesse free, Thine own from Satan's tyranny,

From depths of hell Thy people save, and give them victory o'er the grave.

Rejoice! Rejoice! Emmanuel shall come to thee, O Israel!

In alternative hymnals, the opening line is changed to "O come, O Rod of Jesse's stem, from every foe deliver them that trust thy mighty power to save..." Either way, the rod or root of Jesse signifies the stem from which Jesus would come would be through the lineage of David, the youngest offspring of his less famous father Jesse. The humility of this reference is striking indeed...mentioning Jesse rather than King David. Jesus came in all humility as well, born of a teenage mother, birthed in a simple manger, but with power, majesty, and offering a salvation only He could provide.

Consider in your prayers today that the thought of sending Jesus to earth wasn't a last minute idea of God…it was God's plan from the beginning, foretold in the prophets, and enacted through a very humble lineage. As you pray today, thank God for how intimately acquainted he is with every hair on your head, every concern of your heart, every thought in your mind. Allow the Lord to reign victoriously in your soul, yes even today.

Day 5 – Traditionally read on December 21 – Key of David

O come, thou Key of David, come and open wide our heavenly home,

Make safe the way that leads on high, and close the path to misery.

Rejoice! Rejoice! Emmanuel shall come to thee, O Israel!

The Key of David reference signifies kingly authority; holding the keys to that control of domain that David once held in a geographical and historical setting would now have worldwide influence in Christ. Found in Isaiah 22 and Revelation 3, Jesus is the fulfillment of the Davidic Covenant and the head of the Church in Philadelphia.

So we cry out once more, "Come, yes come even more, Emmanuel" and be with us, guiding, protecting, sustaining, and ruling over our hearts and lives this new Advent season. With prayerful and joyful anticipation, we await your coming once more in the humble manger of hay, and having risen miraculously from the dead, we look forward with heavenly intent to the time you will come again and usher us into glory with you forever!

In response to that life-changing truth...Rejoice! Find joy in God alone...Rejoice! No matter what life delivers today...Rejoice!

Day 6 – Traditionally read on December 22 - Dayspring

O come, Thou Dayspring, come and cheer our spirits by Thine Advent here,

Disperse the gloomy clouds of night, and death's dark shadows put to flight.

Rejoice! Rejoice! Emmanuel shall come to thee, O Israel!

Dayspring is literally "dawn," the physical light of the sun at the start of a new day. At the dawning of light, we welcome Christ into the world to shatter the darkness that had previously plagued the people of God. At long last, the promised One has come to light up the world and cheer our waning spirits. With the dawn, the clouds of night are dispersed and new life emerges from below the horizon... come dayspring, come quickly, so our darkly shadowed world can find freedom and joy in the light of day.

What is the darkness over your heart and life today? What are the heavy concerns that weigh on you, hold you back from the abundant life, and follow you like a dark cloud above? The coming of Emmanuel is a tangible reminder that our dark shadows are put to flight...set free to be released...no longer are you held down in bondage to those heartaches. In Jesus, you are free to live and breathe and have your being fully released in him. Are you willing to hold looser or fully release those dark shackles that tie you down? Freedom in Jesus will transform your soul and will invite you into a deeper trust this Christmas. May it be so.

Day 7 – Traditionally read on December 23 – Desire of Nations

O come, Desire of nations, bind in one the heart of all mankind;

Bid Thou our sad divisions cease, and be Thyself our King of peace.

Rejoice! Rejoice! Emmanuel shall come to thee, O Israel!

As King of all nations, we now anticipate the arrival of genuine peace. In fact, our hearts cry out for such peace each time we celebrate another season of Advent. Why? Because every year of our lives there are wars that hinder our peace...somewhere in the world, and even in our country, community, church, neighborhood, and among family and friends. Every division, whether large or small, is sad...simply sad. There is nothing we desire in times of strife more than peace. Jesus is the author and perfect example of reconciliation…in Him there is peace.

Christmas is coming and our hearts are growing in loving anticipation and joyful celebration. The season of Advent reminds us to simply wait…in due time, in God's time, He sent His Son into the world in an unlikely way through unconventional means and in an unglamorous place. We wait with prayerful hope that once more the worshipful celebration of the coming of Jesus in a humble stable will draw us back home…into the arms of God. And, eventually back home into the arms of others, even those with whom today we are not in peace.

Rejoice, dear brothers and sisters in Christ…Jesus has come in a lowly manger and will come again in triumphant glory. Rejoice! Rejoice! Alleluia! Amen!

Christmas Eve – December 24

Advent waiting, watching and wondering:

embracing the coming of the Christ child

prophetically, humbly and gloriously.

O Come, O Come, Emmanuel!

Rod of Jesse, freeing us from Satan's tyranny victoriously;

Dayspring, dispersing gloomy clouds with cheers on high;

Key of David, opening wide the path to our heavenly home;

Lord of Might, holding firm the Law in majesty and awe;

Wisdom from on high, inviting order on the way to knowledge;

Desire of nations, binding all people in one heart and mind;

Our hymn of praise exalts the heavens and blankets the earth.

O come, O come, Emmanuel…your prophets foretold the truth.

Wonderful, Counselor, Mighty God, Everlasting Father, Prince of Peace;

Emmanuel has come, is with us now, and will come again once more!

What follows are the verses to the hymn, O Come, O Come, Emmanuel, offered in the versions available in English hymnals today:

O come, O come, Emmanuel,
And ransom captive Israel,
That mourns in lonely exile here,
Until the Son of God appear.
Rejoice ! Rejoice ! Emmanuel
Shall come to thee, O Israel.

O come, Thou Rod of Jesse, free
Thine own from Satan's tyranny ;
From depths of hell Thy people save,
And give them victory o'er the grave.
Rejoice ! Rejoice ! Emmanuel
Shall come to thee, O Israel.

O come, Thou Dayspring, from on high,
And cheer us by Thy drawing nigh;
Disperse the gloomy clouds of night,
And death's dark shadows put to flight.
Rejoice ! Rejoice ! Emmanuel
Shall come to thee, O Israel.

O come, Thou Key of David, come
And open wide our heav'nly home ;
Make safe the way that leads on high,
And close the path to misery.
Rejoice ! Rejoice ! Emmanuel
Shall come to thee, O Israel.

O come, Adonai, Lord of might,
Who to Thy tribes, on Sinai's height,
In ancient times didst give the law
In cloud and majesty and awe.
Rejoice ! Rejoice ! Emmanuel
Shall come to thee, O Israel.

O come, O come, Emmanuel!
Redeem thy captive Israel
That into exile drear is gone,
Far from the face of God's dear Son.
Rejoice! Rejoice! Emmanuel
Shall come to thee, O Israel.

O come, thou Branch of Jesse! draw
The quarry from the lion's claw;
From the dread caverns of the grave,
From nether hell, thy people save.
Rejoice! Rejoice! Emmanuel
Shall come to thee, O Israel.

O come, O come, thou Dayspring bright!
Pour on our souls thy healing light;
Dispel the long night's lingering gloom,
And pierce the shadows of the tomb.
Rejoice! Rejoice! Emmanuel
Shall come to thee, O Israel.

O Come, thou Lord of David's Key!
The royal door fling wide and free;
Safeguard for us the heavenward road,
And bar the way to death's abode.
Rejoice! Rejoice! Emmanuel
Shall come to thee, O Israel.

O come, O come, Adonai,
Who in thy glorious majesty
From that high mountain clothed in awe,
Gavest thy folk the elder Law.
Rejoice! Rejoice! Emmanuel
Shall come to thee, O Israel.

Additional verses trans. H. S. Coffin (1916)

O come, Thou Wisdom from on high,
And order all things, far and nigh;
To us the path of knowledge show,
And cause us in her ways to go.
Rejoice! Rejoice! Emmanuel
Shall come to thee, O Israel.

O come, Desire of nations, bind
All peoples in one heart and mind;
Bid envy, strife and quarrels cease;
Fill the whole world with heaven's peace.
Rejoice! Rejoice! Emmanuel
Shall come to thee, O Israel.

About the Author

Stephen A. Macchia is the founding president of Leadership Transformations, Inc. (LTI), a ministry focusing on the spiritual formation needs of leaders and the spiritual discernment processes of leadership teams in local church and parachurch ministry settings. In conjunction with his leadership of LTI, he also serves as the director of the Pierce Center for Disciple-Building at Gordon-Conwell Theological Seminary. He is the author of several books, including *Becoming a Healthy Church, Becoming a Healthy Disciple, Becoming A Healthy Team*, and *Crafting A Rule of Life*. Stephen and his wife, Ruth, are the proud and grateful parents of two grown children, Rebekah and Nathan, daughter in-love Ashley, and granddaughter Brenna Lynn.

For more information about Stephen A. Macchia or
Leadership Transformations, Inc., visit:
www.LeadershipTransformations.org
www.HealthyChurch.net
www.RuleOfLife.com

Other Titles by Stephen A. Macchia

In **Becoming a Healthy Church**, Stephen A. Macchia illustrates how to move beyond church growth to church health. Healthy growth is a process that requires risk taking, lifestyle changes, and ongoing evaluation. This book is a practical, hands-on manual to launch you and your church into a process of positive change. Available in 3 Languages: English, Spanish, Korean.

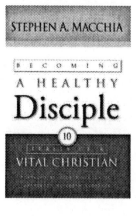

Becoming a Healthy Disciple explores the ten traits of a healthy disciple, including a vital prayer life, evangelistic outreach, worship, servanthood, and stewardship. He applies to individual Christians the ten characteristics of a healthy church outlined in his previous book, Becoming a Healthy Church. Discipleship is a lifelong apprenticeship to Jesus Christ, the master teacher. Macchia looks to John the beloved disciple as an example of a life lived close to Christ.

Becoming a Healthy Disciple Small Group Study & Worship Guide is a companion to Steve Macchia's book, *Becoming a Healthy Disciple*. This small group guide provides discussion and worship outlines to enrich your study of the ten traits of a healthy disciple. This 12-week small group resource provides a Study, Worship, and Prayer guidelines for each session.

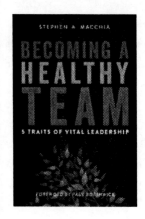

Becoming a Healthy Team is essential for building the kingdom. Stephen A. Macchia offers tried and tested principles and practices to help your leadership team do the same. He'll show you how to Trust, Empower, Assimilate, Manage, and Serve. That spells TEAMS and ultimately success. Filled with scriptural guideposts, Becoming a Healthy Team provides practical answers and pointed questions to keep your team on track and moving ahead.

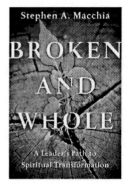

In **Broken and Whole** Stephen A. Macchia offers the gifts of love found in 1 Corinthians 13 as the antidote to our brokenness. He writes with personal transparency from his own experience. Each chapter concludes with a powerful spiritual assessment tool to use in reflecting on our own leadership strengths and weaknesses. By embracing and befriending our own brokenness we can find true wholeness in God's strength. As you progress through the book, you will discover a new way to live in freedom and joy.

In **Crafting a Rule of Life** Stephen A. Macchia looks to St. Benedict as a guide for discovering your own rule of life in community. It is a process that takes time and concerted effort; you must listen to God and discern what he wants you to be and do for his glory. But through the basic disciplines of Scripture, prayer and reflection in a small group context this practical workbook will lead you forward in a journey toward Christlikeness.

Legacy: 60 Life Reflections for the Next Generation will help you capture the wisdom you have gained through years of experiencing the twists and turns of life and record them in a way that makes a great gift for those you love. Not only will they get a window into your heart for them but you might also help them dodge a couple of significant potholes in life. This is a gift that keeps on giving!

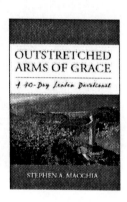

The 40-day Lenten season is typically a time when we choose to abstain from a desire or practice some new measure of devotion. Whether you choose to give something up or take something on (or neither), what's most important is ensuring your heart is attentive to the gifts of grace that Jesus has given by way of his ultimate sacrifice on the cross: forgiveness of sins, fullness of life, and a forever home awaiting for you in heaven. May the journey ahead be good for your soul as you rest in **Outstretched Arms of Grace**.

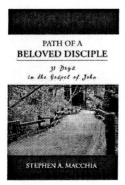

Welcome to the delightful journey of discipleship! Jesus invites us to say an enthusiastic "Yes!" to his beckoning call: Come close, draw near, and follow me. This is exactly what John the Beloved Disciple said long ago and it's our invitation to intimacy today. Becoming a "beloved disciple" of Jesus is the focus of the 31 reflections contained in this devotional guide, **Path of a Beloved Disciple**.

How is your heart condition? In **Wellspring: 31 Days to Whole-Hearted Living** we look at the positive (life-giving) and negative (joy-stealing) conditions of the heart, from both a biblical and relational perspective. With practical applications throughout, this book serves as both a comfort and an inspiration to the reader who longs to reorder their loves for God, his creation, their daily life in God, and their heart for all who cross their path.

Come Home My Soul: 31 Days of Praying the Living Word. When is your heart most at home with God? In prayer ... and the Scriptures are filled with prayers that inspire our soul and become templates for the longing of our heart. The invitation contained in this 31-day devotional is to join your heart with the prayers of God's people, recorded and preserved for us in the richness of the biblical text. Consider each reflection as a pathway that leads your soul back home to the embrace of God, regardless of the season you may be experiencing. Each prayer is offered to us in times of plenty or want, whether fruitful or fallow, hardened or abundant. Join the eternal chorus of prayer and discover afresh the delight of returning once more to your heart's true home.

Additional Resouces @
SPIRITUALFORMATIONSTORE.COM

Guide to Prayer for All Who Walk With God

The latest from Rueben Job, A Guide to Prayer for All Who Walk With God offers a simple pattern of daily prayer built around weekly themes and organized by the Christian church year. Each week features readings for reflection from such well-known spiritual writers as Francis of Assisi, Teresa of Avila, Dietrich Bonhoeffer, Henri J. M. Nouwen, Sue Monk Kidd, Martin Luther, Julian of Norwich, M. Basil Pennington, Evelyn Underhill, Douglas Steere, and many others.

Guide to Prayer for All Who Seek God

For nearly 20 years, people have turned to the Guide to Prayer series for a daily rhythm of devotion and personal worship. Thousands of readers appreciate the series' simple structure of daily worship, rich spiritual writings, lectionary guidelines, and poignant prayers. Like its predecessors, A Guide to Prayer for All Who Seek God will become a treasured favorite for those hungering for God as the Christian year unfolds.

Guide to Prayer for Ministers and Other Servants

A best-seller for more than a decade! This classic devotional and prayer book includes thematically arranged material for each week of the year as well as themes and schedules for 12 personal retreats. The authors have adopted the following daily format for this prayer book: daily invocations, readings, scripture, reflection, prayers, weekly hymns, benedictions, and printed psalms.

Guide to Prayer for All God's People
A compilation of scripture, prayers and spiritual readings, this inexhaustible resource contains thematically arranged material for each week of the year and for monthly personal retreats. Its contents have made it a sought-after desk reference, a valuable library resource and a cherished companion.

LEADERSHIP TRANSFORMATIONS INC.

FORMATION | DISCERNMENT | RENEWAL

- Soul Care Retreats and Soul Sabbaths
- Emmaus: Spiritual Leadership Communities
- Selah: Certificate Program in Spiritual Direction (Selah-West, Selah East)
- Spiritual Formation Groups
- Spiritual Health Assessments
- Spiritual Discernment for Teams
- Sabbatical Planning
- Spiritual Formation Resources

Visit www.LeadershipTransformations.org or call (877) TEAM LTI.